# Leade
# for the Lc



## Affirming the Value of Staying

**Henry Corbett**

Vicar of St Peter and St John Chrysostom, Everton,

Warden of Shrewsbury House and Chaplain to Everton FC

**GROVE BOOKS LIMITED**

**RIDLEY HALL RD CAMBRIDGE CB3 9HU**

# Contents



CPAS is an Anglican evangelical mission agency working mainly in the UK and Republic of Ireland. We enable churches to help every person hear and discover the good news of Jesus Christ. Our vision is to see effective, Christ-like leaders at all levels in our churches: men, women and young people who point others to Jesus. Good leadership is key to church growth and that is why we are investing all our energy in developing leaders.
www.cpas.org.uk.



**First Impression** July 2020
**ISSN** 2041-0972
**ISBN** 978 1 78827 131 8

# Foreword

There is much to commend short- and medium-term ministries.

Christian leaders will often point to St Paul and remark that he made a lasting impact on the life of the church and the wider world without staying in the same place for very long. One almost hears the astonishment in the tone of St Luke when he records that Paul preached in Rome for a full two years (Acts 28.30)! Indeed, the person who breaks up the ground and then plants seeds might not be the one (and might not be meant to be the one) who reaps the harvest. This is because people come into Christian leadership with different personalities and gifts: some with gifts of shaking, unsettling and disturbing while others are gifted at nurturing, encouraging and growing. And contexts differ: sometimes, for example, the necessary work of dismantling unhelpful attitudes and structures can diminish a congregation's willingness to trust a leader to take them on to the next stage of their life, and so it might be right for them to move on after a relatively short period.

In the same way, others will point to Jesus himself, whose whole ministry is delivered in three tumultuous years of miraculous signs and life-giving teaching—and no permanent place of residence. Three years may be long enough, provided the leader is a mighty worker of miracles, has no concern for their reputation, absolute dependence on the Father, unshakeable confidence that everything that is undertaken is the will of God and a readiness to lay down their life.

Undoubtedly there are some difficulties with long-term ministry. Gary McIntosh summarizes a widely held suspicion of long-term ministry, based on interviews with pastors who had remained in post for twenty-five years or more:

> The first ten years were great; the second ten years were good; I should have left in year twenty.[1]

And Paul Rosier noted:

> Change is endemic in every area of life—on average we move house every eight years, change our car every four and a half years and change job every two years. Christian ministry is not immune to change. The average duration of a Church of England ministry is seven years, and in the Baptist Union it is six and a half years. Only one in nine Baptist ministers stays in a particular local ministry beyond 12 years.[2]

As a minister in the Church of England, who has led the same church for 15 years, it has been suggested to me by respected colleagues that I ought to have looked for another post before now. Such comments are offered with a mix of concern and suspicion by those who find it hard to conceive that after a decade and a half there could be more that might be fruitfully done. This counsel and the worldview that underpins it are easily internalized. If professionals in comparable fields are moving every few years; if peers and colleagues consider that 10 years is long enough in the same place and if change is the order of the day all around us, how can the long-term minister secure an equal place at the table? Would not their ministry be more fruitful elsewhere for the simple fact of being seen to be fresh and dynamic?

**How can the long-term minister secure an equal place at the table?**

Grove has sought to illuminate these issues before, with Paul Rosier writing from a Baptist context.[3] While there is much in that excellent booklet that applies across church traditions and denominations, there is something about the Church of England's commitment to parish and place that needs to be part of the conversation concerning length of tenure. In the sprawling suburbs of large cities, middle-class worshippers may drive past half a dozen different churches before arriving at the one of the preferred style; whose vicar preaches the best sermon, whose choir or worship band have the best tunes and where the pews have been retained to preserve tradition or removed to ensure comfort. However, in rural areas and in the inner cities, residents whose grandparents might have been baptized at the parish church often closely identify the church with the local community. This does not necessarily have much to do with a commitment to regular worship. In estate parishes, the vicar may be the only professional who both lives and works on the estate. Other professionals will commute into an estate office but will not expect to bump into clients outside the post office, pub or pawnbrokers. In rural settings, residents may have the freedom to remain in the land of their forebears, but on forgotten estates, because of economic exigencies, the opportunity to move may not arise. There is, therefore, a powerful psychological message to be delivered by the minister who chooses to make that parish, that estate their home. This is the essence of incarnational ministry, incarnational leadership. The distance between the minister and ministered to is narrowed because their problems are the minister's problems; their victories are the minister's victories and their frustrations are the minister's frustrations.

Hence this booklet, which seeks to showcase one occasion when long-term ministry was considered the key to something that was godly and life-giving; an occasion when short-term and even medium-term would not do. It profiles what it feels like to be that incarnational, long-term minister; what it means to earn trust; to be valued as one of us; to be legitimized as the voice of a community; to come to regard an estate as home.

Henry Corbett has ministered in Everton in the Diocese of Liverpool for four decades. This is his story, told in his inimitable voice; a story of how one man pitched his tent among what he came to regard as his people.

It will prompt questions for those seeking a new post. Am I being called to long-term ministry? For those who feel that the end of their current ministry may be approaching, is there yet more fruit to be had? How does this local context speak to me of the need for short-, medium- or long-term ministry?

Greg Smith
Vicar of St Andrew's Church, Eastern Green Coventry

# 1 General Introduction

> You'll only be here 5 minutes and then you'll **** off like the police inspectors, the social workers and all the others...

That was said to me in my early days as an ordained minister in Everton alongside other similar comments to the same effect. Unsurprisingly, such comments stayed with me.

To put it another way: it was the concern of residents in the parish that professionals would come to the area—social workers, police officers—and local people would welcome them, get to know them, help them understand the community and local cultures. Then just when residents felt that maybe these social workers or police understood the community, off they would go to another posting with 'Three years in Everton' on their CV. 'Just as we get to know them, they go off...' locals would say. Or, more telling, 'Just as we think we've taught them our ways they move off and we have to start all over again. We think, "What's the point?" when another person takes over from them. Why can't they stay longer?'

In some cases, of course, local people would be glad to see the back of an unsympathetic social worker or a judgmental police officer and yes, there have been cases of those. 'My job is to get rid of these scrotes any way I can' said one newly arrived police inspector many years ago to a community lunch the church had laid on. That comment damaged relationships and we were glad to see the back of that inspector. I hasten to add that many other police inspectors have been keen to listen, made good links with local community leaders and we were sick to see them move on. Could not the listening, respectful ones stay, especially when they had earned the trust of the community?

In the case of clergy and church leaders it is of course not always right for vicars to stay on in places for a long time (dangers and drawbacks feature in chapter six). Personalities and parishes vary, and short- and medium-term ministries undoubtedly have their rightful place. But the concern of this booklet is to affirm the value of long-term ministries in some, even many, situations. One reason for that, as above, is that it shows a genuine listening ear to the voices of the community. Another reason to value long-term leadership is that for some leaders the option to move is not always present, whether because of lack of opportunity or because their partner may have a job or role in the area that is highly valued, or because children are at an age where to move would be counterproductive, even seriously damaging. For such clergy to feel they are in some way inferior because they are staying rather than moving is not for a moment helpful. 'Are you still there in St X's?' is sometimes said with an unmistakably pejorative tone, as if you are still there because not good or rated enough to move. In some cases, 'Are you still there?' is said with respect and even admiration, but for the former instances this booklet is designed to encourage the leader that long term can have great benefits, for the leader and for the community or communities served. Leadership for the long term can be a very good and positive thing.

# 2 The Backstory

So what is my story?

I came to Everton in inner-city Liverpool in 1978 to work as curate to the rector, Julian Charley. He had succeeded Roger Sainsbury in 1974 and would leave Everton in 1987 (Roger had been in Everton from 1963–1974). Thus there was not a pattern of short ministries, and both Julian's and Roger's ministries and leadership were hugely appreciated by local people. Defining long term is not easy, but Roger's 11 years were not seen as short term, and his time had concluded with the completion of a new St Peter's and Shrewsbury House building.

Julian's own time came to an end during a very difficult, even traumatic, time for the parish. Liverpool City Council had produced a regeneration plan that designated part of the Everton area as a large park, envisaging the demolition of much of the housing. 'When we have decided what to do with Shrewsbury House we will tell you,' we were told. One possibility was for it to house canoes by the lake that was planned! The local West Everton Community Council (WECC) had organized a questionnaire for local residents about the proposed plans for the area. People from St Peter's and from the local Catholic churches were involved in WECC and helped to take the questionnaire round, house by house, flat by flat. The clear response from residents was 85% in favour of keeping the good housing in the area, demolishing the poorly conditioned tower blocks and maisonettes, not having a huge lake with canoes, and keeping the community going with local schools and shops, with a smaller park at the top of Everton hill so that the wonderful view to the city centre, across the Mersey to Wirral and beyond to Wales, would be restored for all to enjoy.

A good number of us from Everton had been down to try and make our voice heard in the consultation about the council's plans for the area, but were told 'You can't build houses on hills' (many houses had stretched up Everton hill for decades) and even 'The vicars and the priests are only interested in more people in their parish so that they can get more money on the collection plate'!

Would anyone listen to the local residents and their views?

**Would anyone listen to the local residents and their views?**

By this time, I was no longer curate but had been appointed as Team Vicar by Bishop David Sheppard. I was also no longer single but in 1979 had married Jane, whom I had met years earlier when we were both helping as volunteers in Shrewsbury House. With Julian leaving, David Sheppard was content both to appoint me as Rector of St Peter's and Warden of Shrewsbury House and also to be totally supportive of Jane's work as a voluntary community activist in the area. It was clear to him, Jane and me, and others in the churches and community, that it was vitally important to keep some continuity of ministry at this very difficult and stressful time. Not to do that would have sent a message out that the church did not understand the pressures on the community and the importance of appropriate leadership, which someone who knew the situation could offer. The community would have been deeply unimpressed at a bishop not valuing the need for continuity in such a situation.

I was installed as Rector of St Peter's and Warden of Shrewsbury House at a service in St Peter's, with three emptied-out tower blocks looming over the church. The congregation were pleased that in Jane and I, people they knew would be continuing to support the fight for our West Everton community. Grace Sheppard attended with husband Bishop David officiating, and Grace delivered soon after a Radio 4 *Thought for the Day* contrasting the bleak grey empty tower blocks outside the church with the warmth and hope of the service inside. Local people felt they had been listened to and that the work of continuing to stand up for what would be best for the area could continue with a couple who knew the situation and the recent and more distant history, and who would work with the people, not at them.

**Local people felt they had been listened to**

I am still Rector of St Peter's, Warden of the 'Shewsy,' (as it is affectionately known) and now also vicar of the neighbouring St John Chrysostom Church Centre in Everton. I also became chaplain to Everton Football Club's training ground, first at Bellefield and now at Finch Farm, a post Julian Charley encouraged me to accept ('It will be good for you to have something outside the parish, something different…'). That chaplaincy has also been long term, stretching back to Howard Kendall's first stint as manager: 'My players may have problems,' he said, 'but they won't always come to me as I'm picking the team. First-team players may be a bit wary of you as they have lots of people wanting a bit of them: so start with the apprentices and then when they are in the first team they will know that you are genuine and trustworthy and can pass that word round to the others.' Wise advice: he did not want my chaplaincy to be short term, just as local Everton residents did not want a listening police officer, social worker, housing officer, GP or vicar to be short term.

# 3 The Importance of Context

I love the Church of England parish system. Every church—Anglican or not—has a community or communities in which they are placed and which, with God's Spirit's help, they will seek to love and serve, but the Anglican church has a responsibility for everyone in a particular geographical area. Wherever you travel in England you are in a parish; there is a church and a vicar, who has a pastoral and evangelistic responsibility for that parish.

Every parish is of course different and has its own distinctive features, culture or, increasingly, cultures. It is certainly not 'one size fits all', 'one style fits all' or 'one length of term of leadership fits all.'

There was an understanding for some Anglicans in days of old that when a minister made it to their incumbency that was where they would serve their ministry until retirement. Such a view had its obvious problems, maybe hinted at in that hopeless word 'incumbency': it sounds as though it is where you lie down and go to sleep. Was that true in some sad cases?! More seriously, not every context or parish lends itself naturally to an extended ministry.

Likewise, whether for reasons of the vicar's liveliness and freshness or because of the parish's need for new leadership, or for other factors such as health, family concerns or responsibilities, long-term ministries clearly do not fit every situation.

## Do long-term ministries fit some contexts?

But do long-term ministries fit some contexts? What if, as in the case of the Everton community in the 1980s, an area is in the midst of extensive, controversial change and turbulence and continuity would be valued by the community? What if short-term ministries communicate all too powerfully a lack of care, commitment and listening?

What if the church community value their minister and leader and want them to stay on after five to seven years, and their reasons are not just selfish and unimaginative ('Better the devil / vicar you know')? What if they feel that their vicar or leader moving on would send out a message of an uncaring church? Would they feel that they are just being used as a stepping-stone for the person's career as the minister moves on 'up' to a 'better' post and situation?

What if the leader of the church has been preaching on the value and importance of every individual from Gen 1.28, a value that insists no one's views should be ignored? The St Peter's Church congregation was in active support of the WECC questionnaire asking for local people's views to be taken on board by the council about the park and the housing demolition because they believed local people's views mattered, not just those of some of the councillors. For their minister to move or be moved without any reference to their views would be a contradiction of their understanding of an application of that verse. An oft-repeated motto in Everton was, 'Who does it affect? Consult them!' Then, after consultation by some groups was not being taken seriously, it became, 'Who does it affect? Involve them' and more recently still the powerful phrase, 'Nothing about us, without us, is for us.' I remember a local person saying, 'We are seen to be the little people as they take their decisions about our area.' She had come to a determined Christian faith that believed that God did not see people that way, and that her views and those of her neighbours should be taken seriously and would contribute to better decision-making.

## Listening to the Local Context

How has that translated into discussions concerning long-term leadership? In 1997, a local Catholic priest was asked after 13 years in Everton to go to a new ministry in Northern Ireland. He had been part of our campaigns for social justice and had been a great advocate for the incorporation of the wisdom and experience of local people in decision-making.

He came to work alongside local people, learning from their wisdom, their culture, their experiences, their priorities. Would those principles count for nothing when it came to his staying or leaving? He chose to consult, involve and listen to local people. He laid out the reasons for his being asked to go to Northern Ireland, explaining the needs of the situation there. We all wanted him to stay but also appreciated the need for his gifts and experience to be used in a seriously worrying situation in Northern Ireland. There was never a feeling that Northern Ireland was a 'better' place than Everton, or that the priest was being promoted up some ecclesiastical ladder. The discussion was about the needs in Northern Ireland and the contrasting needs in Everton and there was an awareness that he had the experience and talents to meet both. In the end he went with our blessing, prayers and support, promising to keep in touch. He believed there could be helpful links between the two communities, a belief he put into practice with some great exchange visits that encouraged both groups.

**When it came to his staying or leaving he chose to consult local people**

If he had just been moved on without any of the above involvement of local people, a message would be heard by many in the community that their view was not important. When he left after 13 action-filled years, our local community newspaper had as its front-page headline, 'Thanks, Father-Mate,' with his reflections and thanks for all he had learnt and experienced in his time in Everton.

# 4 Understanding a Context Can Take Time

I remember it being said at a gathering of ministers, 'When you go to a new church make the decisions you know you will have to make at the start: it will only be more difficult to make them later.' I have always questioned the wisdom of that advice. It seems disrespectful to the people and context you are moving to. The leader who does not take time to listen, to understand the various backstories, to appreciate the tensions, hopes and fears, is a leader who is likely to quickly antagonize local people inside and outside of the church.

Understanding a parish or area and its people is not achieved from a quick briefing from a parish/area profile, written to recruit a new minister. Who put the profile together? What was their agenda? How much did they know about the area and its context? Do they know about what other churches and organizations are doing in the area?

## Responding to Local Needs

In Everton in the 1970s the state of the housing was a strong local concern. The Arkwright estate with its maisonettes and flat roofs was very damaging to residents' health. 'Come and look at my child's bedroom: damp down the walls,' I would be told on visits. The newly built Radcliffe estate may have won an award for its imaginative lay out based on a Cornish village, but local people were not consulted or involved in its design and it soon proved to be a disastrous rabbit warren of an estate. There was no place for a car to be parked anywhere near a house or flat: the idea of parking it outside the estate and walking a distance to your home would not have got approval if the architects had thought to avail themselves of local wisdom. And when the heroin trade came to the estate in the 1980s the warren was perfect for the minority who were dealing such drugs to escape the pursuit of any police officer.

**A church leader could surely not step aside and pass by on the other side**

What should a church leader do in a situation crying out for better housing, for better health, for better safety in the face of illegal drugs that were bringing with them burglaries and gang threats around territory?.Sermons in church spoke of a God who cares about all of life, and a church leader could surely not step aside and pass by on the other side. Vital to effective leadership in that situation is to understand as best you can the true situation, listen to local wisdom, and also crucially to work with others in addressing the situation.

All that can take time. A short-term leader is less likely to appreciate the situation, the issues, the potential allies and the history. In the case of the Radcliffe estate, it was important to work with West Everton Community Council, a group that was resident-led and had the confidence of local people. Then it was important to be at the meeting of residents from the estate to talk about a way ahead. The view from the police was that nobody would come because of intimidating threats from the drug dealers against any who might attend such a meeting. The small group of us who set up the meeting hoped maybe 10 or 12 people would come. Over 100 people bravely attended, and arrived at a consensus that the priority was to address the universally felt housing need, not the more dangerous drug-dealing. Both the Catholic priest and I were involved, along with other Christians from both churches and others with no church affiliation. It was a community campaign with the churches' support, not a churches' campaign, and was all the stronger and more effective for that reason. Those community links and links with other local churches can take time to build up. Another minister with a long-term ministry writes in a letter, 'It was over time that we built deeper relationships with other ministers and their congregations and that enabled us to work more closely on some projects. Over time you engage more deeply with the community and understand how it works better. You develop quick ways of learning information: you get insider information and people trust you to work with them.'

**Over time you engage more deeply with the community**

Another campaign in Everton in the 2000s was to care for a group of asylum seekers from Iraq who had been moved from Kent and placed in two empty tower blocks in the parish. With our community newspaper the *Everton Telegraph* (Everton Telly as it is known), a local Christian, Matt, and I visited in the two blocks. With it being Christmas time the headline was unsurprisingly 'Jesus was an Asylum Seeker,' as we referenced his treatment under King Herod. Some spoke very little English, but we met and chatted with Arkan who spoke good English and whose father, killed under the regime of Saddam Hussein, had told him that 'Christians can be good people.' When conditions in the blocks got worse and the landlady (who was not from the area) was bullying the blocks' tenants not to complain, Arkan rang me. 'Henry, I want to do your church a favour. We want to use it as a sanctuary while we go on hunger strike about the conditions we are living in.'

I had no idea how to respond to that except to say, 'Come round, Arkan, and we can talk about it.' As he and ten other Iraqi asylum-seekers arrived at the vicarage door I had already rung my wife Jane and she had rung our local Member of Parliament, Louise Ellman, who in turn had contacted the local police community relations officer. In the vicarage kitchen we talked together about a way forward, and Arkan and his friends did in fact stay in Shrewsbury House. They came off their hunger strike, thankfully, and they called into church grateful for our hospitality. Louise Ellman took a petition from the local churches to parliament and raised the issue of the ill-treatment of the asylum-seekers. The bullying landlady was disqualified, and the tower blocks were subsequently sold. Sadly, the asylum seekers were moved away against their will from the area they were beginning to feel welcomed in.

What is the point of the story in terms of the value of long-term leadership? Those contacts and our credibility with the MP and the police, built up over a number of years, were invaluable. Would they have visited our kitchen so quickly without that mutual trust and respect earned over a considerable time?

## Trust and Understanding

There was another helpful consequence of Jane and my being in the area long term. In the Everton community there were questions about this sudden influx of asylum seekers: who were they? Were some of the stories in the tabloid papers true? How much money were they getting? What was going on? In the *Everton Telegraph*, I was able to put out the true facts about Arkan and his friends to every home in the West Everton area. I interviewed Arkan in the Shewsy with the young people listening to his story, in which he described the real danger he was in, and they heard his deep-felt gratitude about being safe in Liverpool. The church congregation were quick to welcome him and the group because of their trust in Matt's, Jane's and my involvement with them and our support for them. Such trust is not a given, but long-term leadership can earn such trust, which is invaluable in crisis situations such as 11 Iraqi asylum-seekers going on hunger strike.

**Long-term leadership can earn such trust, which is invaluable in crisis situations**

Another long-term minister has spoken to me about the importance of his being around in the community at times of crisis. When there were frightening riots in his parish, he was able to speak both to the police and to local residents and be a trusted bridge-builder and pastor to both. He was also glad to have been around for some years in the church when there were some tragic suicides, which deeply affected the church membership. At such times an understanding of something of the history, with bridges already built with the participants, the families, those closely involved, is of huge pastoral and missional help.

Another vicar with long-term inner-city experience writes, 'Over time you build trust and understanding; and begin to overcome suspicion. When I first arrived and started walking round the parish in my dog collar I would smile and say hello to people. Some used to cross the road to avoid me! Five or ten years later the same people would cross the road to have a chat. Some even ended up in church. Mutual trust and respect are earned, and that protects you from doing things *to* people rather than *with* them. You engage more deeply with the community and understand better how it works. You develop short cuts for learning information and getting things done. You get insider information. We built deeper relationships with other ministers and their congregations, which in turn enabled us to work more closely together on some projects. People appreciated the fact that they could depend on our presence and contribution: the contribution of our church and other local churches became wanted and valued. This was not just down to our length of stay, but that helped.'

Other professionals have come to similar conclusions. A local GP emphasized the value of his having been in the Everton community for over 20 years because over that time he has got to know his patients, including some with heroin addiction. He has come to understand how in many cases trauma in their earlier years has been a cause of their illegal drug use. He sees them as they come in, not as heroin addicts but as human beings who have this problem in part because of a backstory that he has taken time to understand.

# 5

# Earning Trust

The above examples of community engagement, campaigns and crises where the church has been involved could still work with a short-term leader, a new vicar or minister, but it surely helped that trust had been earned over the years both with church members, the community and with other churches' leaders.

One of the helpful images for me has been the picture of a pigeon on its way to the right destination: instead of flying off immediately in direction A, I was told that the pigeon would circle first, decide which was the right direction and only then, after its circling, would it head off in the correct direction B. As a collaborating leader, in church and community, the process of circling and discovering the relevant people to consult with and involve over a campaign or a church matter is central to my prayers and action. It is also vital to the effective working of the campaign or issue. In the case of the campaign with Arkan, it was important to consult with and involve our local MP, the police, the Shewsy, the church, the young people and other community contacts. Then, with the help of our local community newspaper, we went door-to-door to listen to local residents.

**Long-term leadership removes the need for rush**

Long-term leadership also removes the need for rush and the imposition of plans or presumed answers to questions that require longer consultation. The locally adopted West Everton Community Council motto, 'Nothing about us, without us, is for us,' applies equally helpfully to church matters and decisions. When I became vicar of two parishes— St John Chrysostom, Everton as well as St Peter, Everton—we reached a point when I needed to be at both Sunday morning services and both churches enjoyed the starting time of 11am. After some discussion with both congregations every person in each congregation completed, on their own or with others, a questionnaire as to which time of 10am or 11.30am would suit them best, and in particular to say which time would be impossible for them or to tick 'both' if both were possible. To my relief, in one church there were some for whom only 10am was impossible and some in the other church for whom only 11.30am was impossible. Both church councils could agree the 11.30am for one and 10am for the other. We were all aware that those times were not as ideal as 11am! It took time but everyone was involved.

## Taking Time

A more recent issue for the two churches has been the suggestion of becoming one parish rather than two small inner-city parishes. We had the diocesan planning officer and archdeacon to an initial meeting to look at what would be involved, and a strong voice early on in the discussion said, 'What's the hurry? We need to know more about this and have time to get our heads round it.' Indeed, haste was unnecessary. I was not disappearing in the near future; we could take our time, involve both congregations, see how it had worked well and not so well in other parishes' experience, and after 18 months we reached the point where both parochial church councils agreed to go for it.

The earning and keeping of trust can take time also at the everyday level of personal relationships within the church and outside the church, with individuals, families and friends' networks. A long-term ministry means that you can be at the confirmation of the child you baptized, and you can be at the funeral of the couple you married. You can be filling in the passport form or reference for someone you had in your Shewsy Under 12 football team and who then got caught up in trouble but is now out of prison and is renewing contact with his children. Such continuity earns trust, makes the conversation more engaging and honest and so helps the pastoral ministering. Another person you knew as a teenager in the youth club is in church in his 40s—in part because of positive contact 25+ years before. You understand more of the family networks, the barriers, the openings, the people of peace and the people of not so much peace. You have seen with your own eyes people change. The young person who Jane and I recognized and found stuck trying to climb in through our vicarage window in search of some cash for drugs not only appreciated the mug of tea we gave him after he had extricated himself from the narrow window but came to the Shewsy youth club and never got into illegal drugs again.

**Long-term ministry means that you can be at the confirmation of the child you baptized**

Tragically, other outcomes are not unknown. A quick-witted, gentle character in his teenage years got addicted to heroin and sat some years later in our kitchen with his face battered from punishments for drug debts. A few more years and I was speaking at his funeral. But at that funeral I was able to tell the story of his saying to my daughter Sarah (then a teenager) when she came into the kitchen 'All right, girl, sorry about my face, it's because of those stupid drugs' as he had been beaten up for failing to pay a debt. Then he asked about how she was doing and encouraged her to keep going with her studies and ended 'Don't you get involved in this drugs business.' Sarah learnt two great lessons which she has never forgotten: the illegal drugs business is bad news, and drug addicts are not to be labelled 'smackheads' but can be kind, thoughtful human beings.

Knowing someone and their family over a long period is also obviously a help at their funeral, though I appreciate that a shorter term vicar or leader can do a fine job of speaking about a person after careful, prayerful listening at the pre-funeral visit. But in days when non-religious celebrants are becoming increasingly used by funeral directors one corrective is when the family say, 'We have known this minister for years and we want them to take the service.' Hopefully the service is the better for having someone who knows the deceased, the family, and perhaps important parts of the backstory. A good contact with a family can also help with other occasional offices, such as baptisms when someone you have baptized brings their children for baptism, weddings of people you have known since their childhood and, more rarely but very special, the thanksgivings for 25, 30, 40 years of marriage. Knowing much of the family history, and the family appreciating that, can have great pastoral benefit for all participants.

## Valuing the Long Term

Within the church, the value of—or even just the potential for—a long-term ministry can be important for trust and for wise decision-making. A church that believes its minister and leader is looking for their next move is not likely to be a church with full confidence in that minister's decision-making and their commitment to the mission of that church. Knowing the backstories of your church members in some depth is a firm base for good decisions, enabling their ministries to flourish. A new minister can be more easily taken in by someone eager for power and influence, for less than Christian motives, than the minister who has been around for a while and who is likely to have seen the person in action over an extended period of time. This minister will have a handle on who can give wise advice on their suitability for leadership or a particular ministry. Leadership is very much about enabling and training other leaders. This can take time and is better for having someone who is committed not just for the short term and who has some experience of both the person being considered for a role and the context.

There are also unseen but amusing and valuable perks from a long-term ministry. My earlier correspondent mentioned 'insider information' as being very helpful in engaging with community issues. He also mentions 'insider protection.' He writes:

> On one occasion I took the funeral of the father of a family of lads with whose mother I had worked in a community regeneration programme. The lads were notorious for being in trouble: one of them became a scrap dealer and at the wake after his father's funeral, assisted by a

couple of drinks, he confided in me that he had over time been offered our relatively new camper van by a couple of villains, to whom he had said that I was a sound bloke and to leave me alone!

I have had people offer revenge on my behalf as and when they have been aware of any damage to church or my car (once), or some slight or insult. I have enjoyed turning down the suggestion of retaliation, but been grateful for the concern, arising out of their conviction that here is a genuine person who cares for the community. Such protection involves also the family. When our kitchen window was smashed by two angry young teenagers I discovered who they were and visited their homes, had friendly and positive chats with the father in one case, the mother in the other, and that was the only occasion our windows have been attacked. I knew the two young people, I knew the father and mother, and have kept in friendly contact since.

# 6

# Dangers and Drawbacks

There are of course very clear dangers with a long-term ministry of leadership. Staleness, laziness, getting too comfortable and making assumptions that you know the score when you do not are all very real dangers. Perhaps more important, people in the church and / or community can get disenchanted or bored with you. And at any time, you can drop a brick of such weight that too much damage is done to your reputation or to someone else's, and you need to move for their sake or for yours. If you have been around for some time you may know the way to correct the mistake, but an unredeemable blunder can result in a need to move elsewhere in everyone's interest.

Leaders can stay in a place too long. A friend tells me of his predecessor who reflected that he had stayed too long in that parish: he was there for 18 years but for the last few years his health suffered because of the stress. Leadership can be relentless, our energy levels can sink, and our appetite for necessary new initiatives, for mission and evangelism can fade. Such signs clearly point to the need for rest, a sabbatical, or more. Minister and community colleagues may impart valuable wisdom on the question of whether a short-term breather is required, or whether it may be time to move.

**Staleness and exhaustion are obvious dangers for long-term ministry**

Long-term leadership should always be 'open to move, open to stay,' and an alert leader should be a good listener to themselves, their closest family and friends, and to their colleagues, parish and community. Staleness and exhaustion are obvious dangers for long-term ministry and each person will or should have their ways of staying fresh, energized and with an appetite to learn more of our wonderful God and more about our changing community or communities. There is the need graciously to say 'no' to things that should not be priorities. Being long term in an area can bring an increasing number of issues and people to your door, but being aware of other support systems in the area can help us signpost people to others. And where a good relationship has been built, a 'no' with explanation will be interpreted not as rejection but as 'Ok, Henry, no problem, see you Tuesday,' which protects your breather times. For someone new to the area a 'no' can be misunderstood as rejection and an over-frequent 'yes' to avoid that misunderstanding and to exude willingness to help can cause exhaustion.

We need wise and appropriate strategies to avoid staleness and to remain fresh and energized and with an appetite for worship, fellowship, ministry and mission. Early on as a curate, I was aware that it did not feel good to be tired in the work and of the work and to feel that my mind and spirit's cupboard was bare. My future mother-in-law had warned me of the danger of not eating properly in my busyness. We need also to make sure we are feeding our mental, emotional and spiritual self as well as the physical body. Retreats, sabbaticals, reading weeks, a good spiritual director and good use of ministerial development reviews or appraisals can all be great helps in stocking our cupboard, avoiding complacency and remaining open to our God's leading. For me, along with some of those helps and an annual meet-up with three friends from theological college days, my wife Jane and my children have been great at keeping me thinking, keeping me balanced and making sure I relax, rest, go to a film, have tea and family discussions on anything and everything, and good holidays.

'You owe it to your parish to take your six weeks' holiday a year and a day off each week and to have family time 5–7pm over tea' were instructions from Bishop David Sheppard when I was a curate, 'and if people are surprised by six weeks' holiday you can remind them that many people work five days a week with two days off at the weekend whereas you work six days a week with one day off and that means fifty-two less days off!' You can see I remembered those words and I have always thought I needed to be fresh for ministry rather than worn out by lack of rest or refreshment.

I also believe in recreating on the job, and learnt early on to prepare for a visit with a moment to pray ahead of the visit and think what question would help both them and me. And the more you know the people and agencies in your area the easier it is to know of visits that will inform, stimulate, help and nurture your own needs and thinking, as well as theirs.

In terms of staying alert to the context, in *Built as a City* David Sheppard counselled 'enjoy the area,' and those words too have stayed with me. Every area has its stories, and I have always been keen to understand Everton's history, which has certainly had its many fascinating aspects. It was a delight to help in a small way the local journalist and author Ken Rogers with a chapter of his much-appreciated and best-selling book *The Lost Tribe of Everton and Scottie Road*, and I enjoy too the three-times-a-year challenge of editing the community newspaper we produce from St Peter's and the Shewsy. That keeps me listening to what is stirring up local people. 'What are people angry about?' was a question a Catholic priest told me he would often ask himself as he prayed for his community. This, the Everton Telly, also keeps me in contact with people in the area as it is a great door-opener for contact and conversation, as in the case of asylum seeker Arkan.

Each of us is different in temperament and interests, and different things will energize or exhaust us. For me key elements include: the two home groups I go to each week, studying a passage of Scripture and sharing our experiences, insights and questions, the monthly film I go to with Jane after a careful check of film critic Mark Kermode's review to ensure that our viewing will reenergize us, the visits to people who will help me learn about their lives and how God is at work in them, the annual course on how the Christian faith makes sense and my preparation for that through listening, film, reading and visiting, and the persistent challenge of ministry and leadership in ever-changing inner-city Everton. These all keep me from feeling stale. In the last few years there has been the challenge of digital media and the need to develop useful and engaging ways to use social media to help the church in fellowship and mission as increasing numbers go online (especially, for example, during the coronavirus crisis lockdown) for their information and communication.

Having mentioned family as a huge help and support to me in a long-term ministry, I should add that family can of course be a reason to move. A minister's child was having a terrible time in the local school and he and his wife took the right choice to move to another very different parish at the other end of the city. A minister's partner may have an extremely important job offer that strongly suggests a move, just as a partner's job or ministry or situation may be an important reason to stay. An ageing parent may need their minister son or daughter to move nearer to them, just as children may need some stability rather than too many moves during their school lives. Remaining fresh is a challenge. Over time it is all too possible to get in a rut, get tired of doing the same old things, facing the same challenges and responding to the same people. There is the danger of getting set in particular ways of thinking, working, relating, and of making assumptions that miss the mark because situations and cultures have changed.

## Responding to Change

Nearly every area and context is slowly or quickly changing all the time and I have found staying in Everton far from a stale experience. The area has changed considerably over the 40 years I have been there and even if the area had not lost two estates and ten tower blocks and gained Everton Park with its fabulous view, the people and their thinking, their hopes and fears, would have changed. In a leader's ministry, awareness of those changes in people and culture is important alongside the changes in the streets and environment.

Each autumn I enjoy offering a free accessible apologetics course, with time to discuss the questions people may have about the Christian faith. The opportunity to hear about and discuss the truth or otherwise of Christianity was central to my journey to faith and I love to offer that to others. My first course in 1999 was entitled 'A Faith for the Millennium?' and ran in our local Adult Education Centre. The course was for 10 weeks to coincide with other courses on offer. At tea break the participants on the different courses would meet up. I was delighted that our course was thought to be a great idea and drew as many people as the other most popular course, the salsa dancing! Sadly, the adult education centre closed through lack of funding and the building was knocked down. However, encouraged by the response I have continued to do an apologetics course each year, in different venues, using relevant film clips and other visuals, diagrams, quotations etc. Every year the questions and issues vary, the examples and film clips I use vary, the group changes with now between 10 and 20 people coming to a course that is shortened to 3 weeks to fit people's felt busyness and ambivalence about a longer course. What it does is keep my thinking about the most important questions regarding the Christian faith fresh: is there a God? Is there any evidence? Who is this Jesus? Why is there so much injustice, so many sad stories alongside love, joy, and the great stories? What is life about?!

Staying in a long-term leadership role can also keep your preaching fresh. You cannot dig out the series of sermons you preached on Romans in your last church and embark on them in your new one, as one vicar I was on placement from college with cheerfully did. He moved parishes regularly and each new church got his well-researched series of sermons on Romans and it worked for him and them. But if you stay in a church long term you cannot just repeat sermons. You need to approach the text or passage or book or theme with eyes fresh to see what the writer is getting at and be eager to communicate that into the ever-new situation that the congregation is facing in their varying contexts. As the writer of the Book of Jonah is tilting at racism, then a sermon on Jonah will be grimly relevant to two racist attacks in the area that many in the congregation will know about. If Nehemiah was keen to encourage prayer, perseverance, teamwork and canny strategy in the face of opposition, then that message is relevant to community and church campaigns that face discouragement and opposition. The prophets Amos and Jeremiah challenge a whole system that is creating injustice and is bolstered by complacency, and it is easier for a preacher to be bringing those prophetic messages when they have earned some trust and credibility. Archbishop Desmond Tutu speaks of the need for Christians to address the upstream as well as the downstream issues; yes, to pull people out of the river and offer them a towel and hot drink (the foodbank equivalent), but also to ask the question as to who or what is pushing them into the river. Finding the answers to that vital question may need time, consultation and careful listening to Scripture but also to those most caught up in the contemporary situation. In the gospels Jesus took thirty years experiencing life in Galilee before he embarked on his preaching, teaching, healing and training ministry. What parables from everyday life he told!

# 7 Concluding Thoughts

I am not arguing that everyone should go for long-term ministry or that long-term leadership is always best. Not at all. There are different contexts, different leadership styles and appropriately varying lengths of time. But I am keen to propose that listening to local people, within the church and outside the church, should be part of a leader's discernment process and of their bishop's or church overseer's discernment. Not to do so is to discount the wisdom of people made in God's image and to marginalize them in a decision that very much affects them.

I came to Everton to love and to serve, to listen and to lead, and to live out and share the greatest news in the world. I knew in my thoughts and prayers that the local people should be listened to, by politicians taking decisions about the area and also by church leaders taking decisions about the church's leadership. When my friend and local Catholic priest was asked to move to Northern Ireland, I appreciated the way he wanted to consult with and involve the local community in Everton that he had come to serve. I was saddened when I heard many years ago of a friend who had been moved out from his post in a parish against his and his family's wishes and the wishes of the congregation and community; in fact they were never consulted or involved in the decision but simply told that in the reorganization there was no place for him. I was sad to hear from a vicar who served for many years in one parish that he felt his long stay was not valued by the hierarchy in the church: he had turned down offers to work in cathedrals and had loved his time in the one parish, and exercised there an outstanding, much-appreciated ministry.

And though of course it can often be right to move, I firmly believe that it is also often right to stay. Under 'Latest Vacancies in our Diocese,' a diocese I much love and respect wrote, 'We have put this together as part of our commitment to support our clergy seeking further opportunities to develop their ministry.' I would want to add, 'We fully appreciate that in many cases staying in their situation can also help clergy richly develop their ministry.' And not just develop their ministry but also develop the ministry and mission of others in the parish as they are increasingly trusted, valued and used as leaders of mission together with others in our ever-changing contexts and cultures.

Communities often value stability and continuity: long-term leadership offers that. Church congregations and local communities deserve to have their voice heard—not as the last word, because not every congregation or community will reflect God's priorities—but nor should their views be sidelined. Christian leaders are not individuals on the steps of a career ladder but servant leaders and enablers in ministry and mission in a context, for short or long term.

# Afterword

Henry Corbett's story is a powerful testimony to the faithfulness of one man serving in a particular context; serving men, women and children with God's love. Henry's commitment to long-term ministry is an expression of that love. His explication of how love expresses itself in a willingness to listen and learn is redolent of Christ on the road to Emmaus (Luke 24). Jesus opens with the question, 'What's it like for you?' and listens carefully before unpacking Scripture and revealing the reality of the resurrection. The two disciples in turn realize that Jerusalem remains the place they need to be.

There are many reasons why a leader might leave a church. Rowan Williams writes of St Benedict's 'summons to stability,' alerting us to the current national narrative that embraces our relationship with the EU and attitude to asylum seekers and maintains that everything would be much better if only we could distance ourselves from others.[4] Henry Corbett encourages us, by contrast, to ask ourselves, 'When the going gets difficult, should I stay?'

## Questions to Ponder

- What is the context I am in? Am I growing in understanding it?
- Does the context suit a shorter or long-term leader?
- What is my expectation of the length of time I will serve in my current post given the above context and my own gifts, personality and situation?
- What are my underlying assumptions that lead me to think this?
- How are the powers that be (diocese, district, circuit, Baptist Union etc) likely to view this?
- How might the congregation and leadership team view this (and have I asked them)?
- How might the wider community, including fellow professionals, view this?
- If I were to stay 5 years longer, how might all this change?
- What are the things I might do for God if I move? And what are the things I might do for God if I stay?

Greg Smith
Vicar of St Andrew's Church, Eastern Green Coventry

# Notes

1 Blog post 14 June 2013, https://www.biola.edu/blogs/good-book-blog/2013/long-pastoral-tenure-can-hurt-your-church

2 Paul Rosier, *Long-term Ministry: 'Help, I'm Being Called to Stay!'* (Grove Pastoral booklet P144).

3 See Paul Rosier, *ibid*.

4 Rowan Williams, *The Way of St Benedict* (London: Bloomsbury, 2020) p 27.